A CHILDRENS HUNTING QUIET BOOK

ON THE
HUNT

with Sommer Willis

For my Dad, who shared and instilled in me his love of hunting and the outdoors at a young age.

For my oldest daughter Paetyn who, out of boredom on her first deer hunt, asked me in anguish why she had to "sign that thing" (her hunting license).

-XO

ISBN: 979-8-218-08403

ON THE HUNT

A QUIET HUNTING ACTIVITY BOOK FOR
IN-THE-STAND BOREDOM-BUSTING

Sommer Willis

LISTENING
to the world around you

Be very still and listen carefully.
Write down the sounds you hear in the graph along with
what you think they are, the direction they came from,
and how far away you think they are.

SOUND	ID	DIRECTION	DISTANCE
(ex: "boom")	(ex: "thunder")	(ex: "behind me", or "west")	(ex: "nearby" or "far")

White-tailed deer can also see movement very well.

If we want to see one, we have to sit very still.

THIS BOOK BELONGS TO:

....

and I am hunting with my:

....

Nice to meet you!

You are probably here because someone who loves you very much wants to share their passion for hunting with you. This is a very special time because you are learning skills and making memories that will last a lifetime. Along with being a fun sport, hunting also provides us with food, teaches us about animals and their environment around us, and gives us an opportunity to conserve it.

I started hunting with my dad when I was around your age. He taught me so many things and I can't wait to share them with you during our hunt together.

White-tailed deer can hear very well and are very shy.

If we want to see one, we can't let it hear us.

To be good hunters we must be very quiet and listen.

While you are hunting you may hear a lot of different sounds.

DANTE CAN EVEN CHANGE
HIS DIRECTION MID-FLIGHT.

DANTE CAN GLIDE FOR
UP TO **10** METERS OR **32** FEET
IN A SINGLE FLIGHT!

Wait! He can't see!

Add his eyes and color him in!

Wearing camo helps us
blend in with our
surroundings.

Are you wearing camo?
If so, color it!

To be good hunters, we must look, too.

Even the smallest flicker could be a sign of something important.

SEEING
the world around you

Stay alert and watch closely.
List the objects and animals you see in the graph.

ANIMAL/OBJECT	DESCRIPTION	ACTIVITY	OTHER
(ex: "squirrels")	(how many, what color)	(ex: "eating acorns")	(ex: "chasing each other")

This is what it looks like from my deer stand through my binoculars.

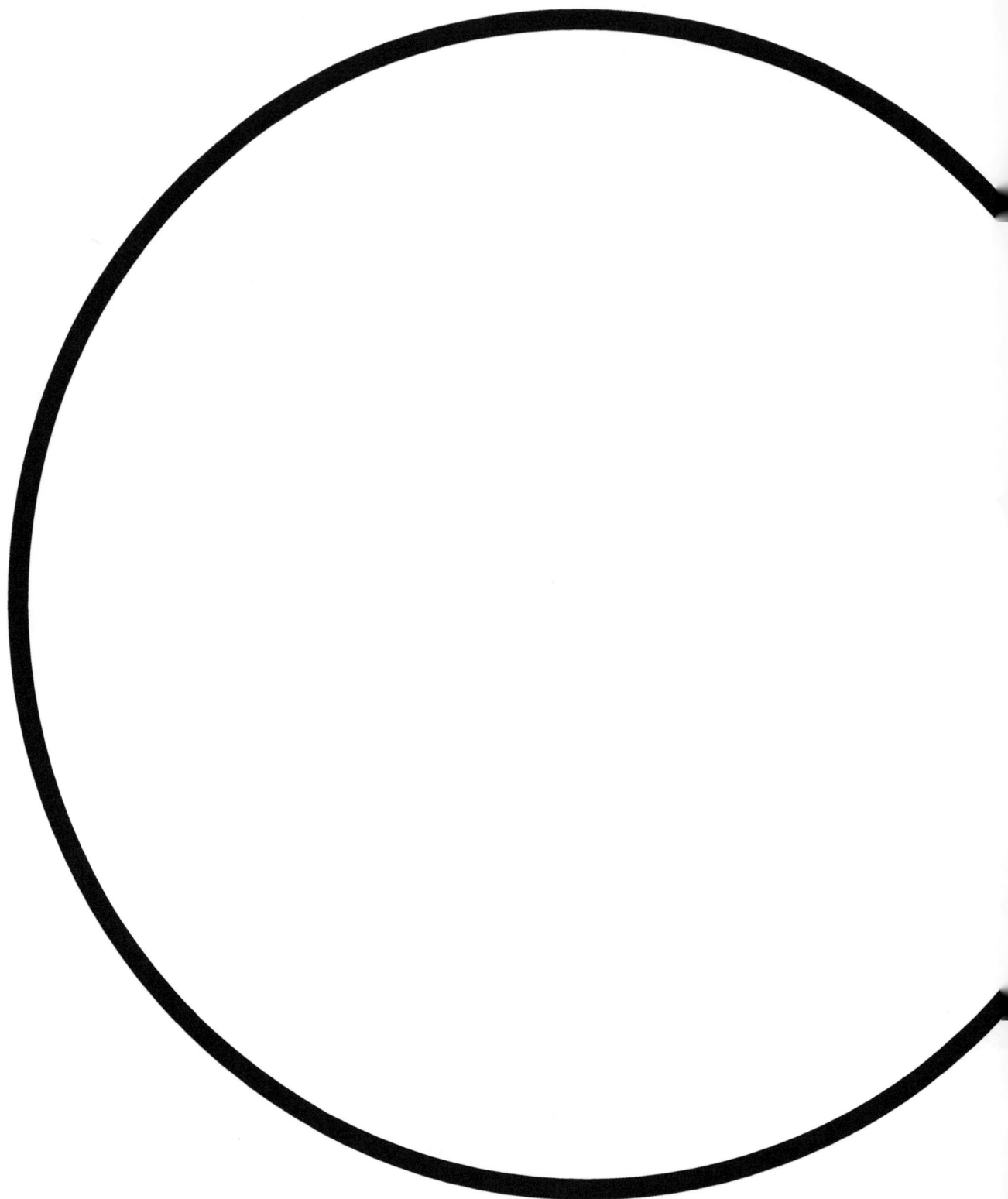

Look through your **BINOC**

ULARS

and draw what you see!

ANIMALS

ARE

ALL

AROUND US

OTHER THINGS YOU MIGHT SEE

(CHECK THEM OFF AS YOU FIND THEM!)

Leaf	Log	Butterfly
Pinecone	Squirrel	Bug
Bird	Ant Mound	Ant
Mushroom	Acorn	Tree

LEARN THE TRACKS

Did you know each of these animals leave footprints behind?
Get to know them so you can see what animals are in your neck of the woods!

(have a pointier tip than hogs and have dewclaws)

(look like good grabbers)

(claws always out)

(tip more rounded than deer)

(claws retracted)

MATCH THE TRACKS

Draw a line to match the animal with its tracks.

HUNTING WORD SEARCH

X	A	I	L	E	A	V	E	S	S	B
H	U	I	R	T	O	D	L	O	P	U
U	T	R	E	F	Q	O	W	E	S	C
N	U	E	E	C	I	E	S	F	A	K
T	M	T	N	D	M	H	U	A	F	L
I	N	O	F	A	W	N	N	E	E	R
N	B	R	M	C	B	R	S	L	T	S
G	I	L	L	O	U	G	H	O	Y	P
A	H	L	T	R	D	I	I	U	M	I
B	A	E	E	N	D	E	E	R	L	K
F	S	E	A	N	I	K	P	M	U	E

AUTUMN	FAWN	DOE	SPIKE
FALL	BUCK	SAFETY	DEER
LEAVES	ACORN	HUNTING	LEAF

TRACE THE LETTERS AND COLOR THE PICTURE

deer

deer deer deer

deer deer deer

FINISH THE BUCK!

(and color him in!)

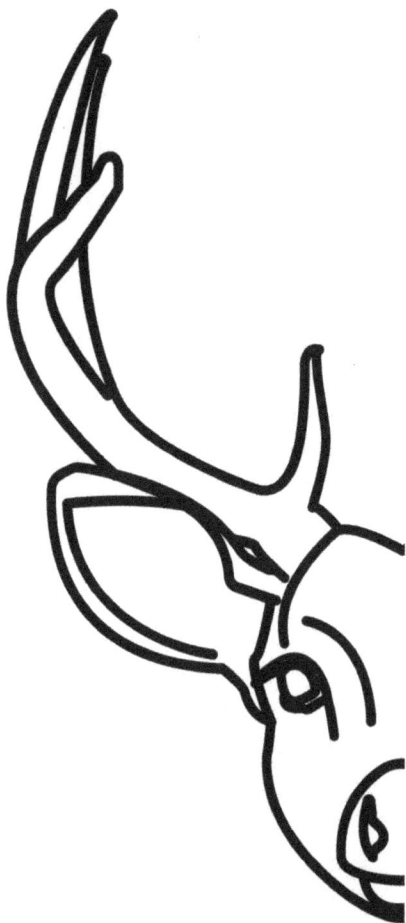

DEER STAND BINGO

During your hunting trip have you or your hunting guide come across any of these items? If so, use a pencil or crayon to mark the items you've seen. The first one with five in a row wins!

acorn	deer feeder	tent	jacket	ATV
rifle	corn	pinecone	hat or cap	gloves
binoculars	squirrel	FREE SPACE	leaf	camo shirt
backpack	sign	turkey	deer	deer call
RV	owl	fire	boots	spider

WHITE-TAIL DEER DEVELOPMENT

Stage: Fawn
Facts: Newborn deer. Stays with Mommy. Has spots.

Stage: Yearling
Facts: 14-18 months old. Begins losing its spots.

Stage: Doe
Facts: Adult female deer. Uses her tail as a signal for danger.

Stage: Buck
Facts: Adult male deer. Has antlers. Coat is reddish-brown in the summer and grayish-brown in the winter.